LIVING EUCHARIST

COUNTER-SIGN TO OUR AGE
AND
ANSWER TO CRISIS

by: Rev. George W. Kosicki, C.S.B.

Faith

Edited and Published by:
FAITH PUBLISHING COMPANY
P.O. Box 237
Milford, OH 45150

Published by Faith Publishing Company

Copyright © 1991, Faith Publishing Company

Library of Congress Catalog Card No.: 91-071543

ISBN: 0-9625975-9-7

TABLE OF CONTENTS

Date	Title of Letter	Page
2/26/90	The Eucharist: a Radiance of God's Mercy and Humility—the Answer to the Crisis in the Church	1
4/23/90	The Crisis over "This is My Body"	4
2/27/90	Eucharist: the Ultimate Humility of God	7
2/28/90	Eucharist: the Ultimate Mercy of God	9
3/01/90	Eucharist as Presence	11
3/02/90	Eucharist as Sacrifice	14
3/03/90	Eucharist as Communion	18
3/16/90	The Action of the Mass	21
3/17/90	Eucharist Prefigured in the Old Testament	24
3/19/90	The Radiance of the Eucharist	27
3/20/90	A Eucharistic Parable	30
3/21/90	Mary, Mother of the Eucharist	33
3/29/90	An Example of Living Eucharist	36
1/04/91	Holy Eucharist	41
1/18/91	The Spiritual Energy of the Eucharist	44

DEDICATION

To Donna and Vinny Flynn, to whom these letters were written.

ACKNOWLEDGMENT

To Bernard Banks, for the cover design.

INTRODUCTION

Exactly what is the EUCHARIST? Is it truly the "real presence?" Or is it "symbolic" of the Body of Christ?

The Eucharist and the Mass are fundamental to the Catholic faith. There is no middle ground, nor room for interpretation. These beliefs are rooted in Scripture, in the words of Jesus Christ.

Today, in this period of watered-down faith resulting from Vatican II misinterpretations, some argue against these beliefs. I recall one modern day "Catholic intellectual" who referred to Adoration of the Blessed Sacrament as, "bread watching." Our Lord must be immensely pleased at how far our great society has progressed.

Others have been a little more discreet. Hans Kung and Richard McBrien, left-wing theologians, seem to say that Jesus did not directly found a Church, or institute Sacraments. According to Kung, the Last Supper was just a meal of celebration, a form of feast—since he expected the end soon. Further, Jesus did not found a Church, nor require any membership in one.

Today, it is not unusual to find theologians (and the ordained), promoting the reception of Holy Communion by anyone and everyone, presumably in the name of "Ecuminism." Of course, since sin hardly exists anymore, this cannot be sacrilegious. It's all in the form of community sharing and celebration. Even the "first Confession" is often times not required for children as a prerequisite to their first Communion. Any and all are seemingly ready to partake.

Has the mysterious, omnipotent power and holiness of The Lord truly been eliminated from our needs? Is His grace, His presence, no longer necessary for our salvation? Does our contemporary society really excuse reverence in the name of freedom of expression?

Down through the generations, the Catholic faithful adhered to definite practices of reverence regarding the Eucharist and partaking in Holy Communion. Many remember the "fast from midnight on," before attending Mass on Sunday morning as a prerequisite to receiving Communion. Is God less Sacred, less Holy, today? And it was clearly understood that being in the state of sin meant that one should not receive the Eucharist? Preparation was required! Reconciliation was needed! The Lord was to be present!

"Forty Hours Devotion" was a feast, a celebration, a time of reverence before the Lord. Bread watching?

To many, there has been a great loss in the liturgical, the ceremony, the reverence of Catholic formality. The mystery associated with the Omnipotent God is being replaced with folk Masses, liturgical dance and a myriad of lay pastoral positions, committees and activities, very few of which are focused on Him who created our existence, on Him who continuously offers His life for our redemption. Does He no longer require our holiness, our reverence, our adoration, our recognition that He is our God?

Mother Teresa expressed some thoughts on it:

"We cannot separate our lives from the Eucharist; the moment we do, something breaks. The Eucharist involves more than just receiving; it also involves satisfying the hunger of Christ. He says 'Come to me.' He is hungry for souls. Nowhere does the Gospel say: 'Go away,' but always 'come to me.' . . . The Eucharist is connected with the passion. If Jesus had not established the Eucharist we would have forgotten the crucifixion . . . To make sure that we do not forget, Jesus gave us the Eucharist as a memorial of His love."

In this book, LIVING EUCHARIST, Fr. George Kosicki provides some interesting answers and insights. He delves into the mystery of the Eucharist, albeit the mystery, like the Blessed Trinity, is beyond our total comprehension. Still, a new awareness, a new insight based on Scripture and Church doctrine, is brought forth with great clarity. Here we see the Eucharist as the epitome of God's Divine Mercy, the ultimate act of humility and love.

During 1990, Fr. Kosicki compiled a series of meditations in letter form, addressed to close friends, Donna and Vinny Flynn. These meditations comprise the text of this book and each of them lends itself to additional meditation on the part of the reader. **Presence, Sacrifice** and **Communion** are the components of the "Living Eucharist." With great faith and simple testimony, the author gives strong evidence that the Eucharistic Celebration is truly the answer to the crisis of our present age.

Fr. George Kosicki, long an advocate of the "Divine Mercy" as promulgated by Sr. Faustina, has recently initiated the APOSTLES OF DIVINE MERCY apostolate in Steubenville, Ohio. As these meditations attest, the Eucharist and Divine Mercy are intimately entwined. May the reader grasp a new and profound appreciation of this miraculous gift, given by Our Lord at the Last Supper.

Bill Reck
Faith Publishing Company

I. THE EUCHARIST—A RADIANCE OF GOD'S MERCY AND HUMILITY—
THE ANSWER TO THE CRISIS IN THE CHURCH

February 26, 1990
Emmaus House

Dear Donna and Vinny,

May the merciful and Eucharistic Heart of Jesus fill you with a new and deeper awareness of His presence in your hearts.

For a number of years I've wanted to write my reflections on the Eucharist. I've written in bits and snatches on the Eucharist as presence and as a healing sacrament; also on Sister Faustina's devotion to the Blessed Sacrament. But a growing desire and urgency have brought me to a Lenten resolution— write for one hour a day. This "penance" for Lent has a two-fold aspect to it. One is to actually sit down and take time to write each day, and the second aspect is to limit myself to just one hour per day and not more. When I get started on a topic I get carried away, so the penance is to stop at one hour.

I just finished offering the votive Mass of the Holy Spirit for the intention of the "Apostles of Divine Mercy" and I want to write in close union with the Eucharistic Lord. What is uppermost on my heart and mind? *The Eucharist is the ultimate and extreme humility and mercy of the Lord Jesus Christ present among us, radiating His merciful love to all who come in humble and obedient faith.* He radiates His mercy by His **presence**—as we come to adore and worship Him, through His **sacrifice**— as we offer ourselves and the whole world in union with Him to the heavenly Father, and in **communion** with Him as we are united and transformed by Him, and so transform the world.

1

I ask you to read that again because it is the statement of my thesis. There is so much in those two sentences that I need to take many a chapter to explain and explore the meaning and truth of what the Eucharist really is—especially in our present times of Eucharistic crisis. Rather than develop the thesis in this letter, I will look at the crisis in the Church experience, primarily in our continent, in order to set the stage for later letters.

How would I characterize our present generation? As one whose concern is for independence and a popularized, so-called democracy. There is great value on a person's freedom to do what he wants and think and express what he feels. I call it the "spirit of 1776", a rebellious independence and a claiming of personal infallibility, so that we have a "plurality of infallibility". The result is confusion in the teaching of some theologians on the nature of the authority of the Church's magisterium, and consequent confusion in loyalty and obedience to the magisterial and even the infallible teaching of the Church.

How does this express itself in terms of the Eucharist? I would describe the current situation in the Church as a "crisis of the Eucharist". Some theologies and practices do not acknowledge the presence of the Body and Blood, Soul and Divinity of the Lord Jesus Christ. There is no need to list the many practices and attitudes that have become prevalent since the Second Vatican Council, because we are already aware of them. But what is necessary, is to point out the drastic effect that various theological teachings and practices have had in so many of our seminaries since 1965. The Eucharistic presence is not prominent; it is not worshipped and reverenced; it is not integrated into the spiritual formation of priests.

The results are obvious. Priestly vocations have bottomed out. The people of God are confused and are suffering.

If all three of the essential aspects of the Eucharist—the sacrament of presence, sacrifice, and communion (John Paul II, *Redemptor Hominis*), are not integrated into the teaching and practice of the priest, then what is our Catholic ministerial priesthood about? What is our baptismal priesthood of the lay faithful about? How can we consecrate the world to God? (See *Lumen Gentium*, # 34)

I see that the answer to the crisis within the Church is in a new and renewed Eucharistic life, a life renewed by the radiance of the Eucharistic Lord that will penetrate our indifference, confusion and lack of faith. One that will confront our sinfulness, breaking down the opaque barriers of our "rebellious independence" and "plurality of personal infallibility". It will be His extreme humility in the Eucharist that will confront our pride; it will be His extreme mercy that will penetrate our self-sufficient independence and radiate through us out to the whole world, so desperately in need of His mercy.

Well, my hour is up! I'll continue in the next letter. I need to start practicing my Lenten resolution so that I'm into the swing of these letters by Ash Wednesday.

> In Jesus, our humble and
> merciful Lord,
> Father George

II. THE CRISIS OVER "THIS IS MY BODY"

April 23, 1990
Feast of St. George
Eden Hall

Dear Donna and Vinny,

May the merciful Lord give you a deeper experience of what it means to be a member of the body of Christ.

As I said in the first letter, "This is a rebellious age." The cry of rebellion is against God. It is a cry of independence and self-determination, most poignantly heard in support of the stance over the issue of abortion. How often we hear the assertion that "I have a right over my body!"

This rebellious cry is a cry against the Lord; it is a cry in contradiction to the Eucharist. The Lord says over us: "This is **my** Body." But so many are rejecting His sovereign reign over us and say, "No, this is **my** body!" And so we are in a crisis of Eucharist.

The Lord made His attitude and position very clear in regard to sexual immorality in St. Paul's first letter to the Church of Corinth. How much more His words apply to abortion! St. Paul speaks in words that have an ironic resonance in our present crisis:

> *Everything is lawful for me—but that does not mean that everything is good for me ... The body is not for immorality; it is for the Lord, and the Lord is for the body. God who raised up the Lord will raise up by this power ... Do you not see that your bodies are members of Christ?* (I Cor 6:12-15)

What St. Paul goes on to say of the sin of fornication as a

4

sin against the body is even more true of abortion:

> *Shun lewd conduct. Every other sin a man commits is*
> *outside the body, but the fornicator sins against his own*
> *body.*   (I Cor 6:18)

Finally St. Paul makes clear the holy nature of our bodies:

> *You must know that your body is a temple of the Holy*
> *Spirit, who is within—the Spirit you received from God.*
> *You are not your own. You have been purchased at a great*
> *price! So glorify God in your body.*   (I Cor 6:19-20)

"So glorify God in your body!" What a clear and contradictory statement to the present crisis of world-wide abuse of the woman's body. And the abuse is world-wide and staggering in its proportions.

The present world-wide number of abortions each year is conservatively reported as forty million (*Review of Inducted Abortions*, Vol. 6), and is possibly as high as sixty million. The impact of this number of abortions was impressed upon me while visiting Auschwitz, the Nazi concentration camp outside of Cracow, Poland.

It was the Monday after the celebration of Mercy Sunday, at the Shrine of Divine Mercy at Lagiewniki, where Sr. Faustina Kowalska is buried. We drove an hour through freezing rain to the town of Auschwitz and entered the camp, now a historic museum, passing under the arch over the entrance. On the arch, a sign in German greeted us: "Arbeit macht frei!" (Work makes for Freedom!) As we gazed at the stockpiles of shoes, suitcases, eyeglasses, women's hair and the reconstructed rooms, I kept praying the words of the Chaplet of Divine Mercy: "Have mercy on us and on the whole world." As I gazed in amazement at the execution wall, at the cell where St. Maximilian Kolbe was starved and finally killed by an injection of phenol, and then at the gas chambers, I didn't know whether to pray or cry.

Then the realization of our present age impressed itself on my mind. Which is worse? Hitler's age in which some four million were killed at Auschwitz and another six million at other camps over a decade—or the decade under Stalin in which he killed, according to Zbgniew Brzerzynski (in *The Grand Failure* of *Communism*), some thirty to fifty million? In the past decade we have surpassed that age by ten-fold: four hundred to six hundred million! More than the population of all of North America, that is, Canada, the United States and Mexico, with Australia and New Zealand added in.

This means that some 125,000 abortions are performed each day! This is one-half the number of conceptions in the world! We are annihilating the human race. We have broken the body of Christ on earth again!

We are in a crisis of Eucharist!

The answer to the crisis **is** the Eucharist—the ultimate humility and mercy of God.

In the Eucharistic Lord,
Father George

III. EUCHARIST, THE ULTIMATE HUMILITY OF GOD

February 27, 1990
Emmaus House

Dear Donna and Vinny,

May the merciful Lord reveal His humble presence in your hearts.

Before me on the desk I have two icons, one of Christ crucified, with Mary and John standing beside Jesus, and the other of the torso of Jesus in the tomb with the title "Extreme Humility". These two icons make present the extreme dimensions of Christ's incarnation, showing how far He would go to show His merciful love for us sinners. The Word of God not only took on flesh from the Virgin Mary by the power of the Holy Spirit, identifying Himself with our humanity in all its sin and weakness, but He went even further. He emptied Himself because He was God, even of His Godhead to become a slave condemned to death, death on a cross (Phil 2:5-11). In extreme humility He was laid in the tomb descending to the dead (Sheol).

The icon of the cross, portraying the scene of John (19:25-37), makes present the reality and grace of the totality of the gift of Jesus, giving us His very life, handing over His Spirit, giving us His mother as our mother, giving us His priesthood in the person of the beloved disciple John, and pouring forth His mercy in the blood and water from His pierced side. In His humility, could He give more?

Yes, He did give more!

The night before He died, gathering His disciples for the paschal meal, He showed His ultimate love for them. He took bread, blessed it, broke it, and gave it to His disciples saying, *"take this all of you and eat it. This is my Body which will be given for you."* Then after the supper He took the cup of wine, blessed it, and gave it to His disciples saying, *"Take this, all of you, and drink from it: This is the cup of my blood, the blood of the new and everlasting covenant. It will be shed for you and for all so that sins may be forgiven. Do this in memory of me"* (Eucharistic Prayer of the Roman Rite).

This is the gift of **ultimate** humility. The living God not only became a man and died for us that we might die and rise with Him—but in His ultimate humility, He left us Himself under the visible signs of bread and wine. In his ultimate humility, He continues to be present with us in His Body and Blood, Soul and Divinity, uniting our sacrifices offered with His, giving Himself to each of the faithful as a communion of merciful love in order that we may be transformed into living Eucharist, His mystical Body.

How humble can God be? God is humility itself. In the Eucharist we experience that humility.

This gift of the Eucharist is **the** countersign to our present age. This ultimate humility of God stands in confrontation to all the rebellious independence, self-fulfillment, luke-warm indifference, pleasure seeking, and pride. The Lord's response to all of this is His humble, silent and hidden presence in the Eucharist. Here is the radiant strength to stand firm in the continual daily passion and crucifixion of the Church, His mystical Body, as we the faithful receive and adore our crucified and risen Lord and Savior.

The ultimate humility of God is the measure of the dimensions of God's merciful love for us. The greater the humility, the greater the mercy. *"There is no greater love than this: to lay down one's life for one's friends"* (John 15:13). The Lord Jesus did just that in giving Himself to us in the Eucharist; He loved us with the greatest love. Can we do any less than fulfill His command:

> *A new command I give to you, that you love one another; even as I have loved you, so you also should love one another.* (John 13:34)

In the humble
Eucharistic Lord,
Father George

IV. EUCHARIST, THE ULTIMATE MERCY OF GOD

February 28, 1990
Ash Wednesday
Emmaus House

Dear Donna and Vinny,

Praised be the merciful Lord Jesus Christ!

In the letter on the Ultimate Humility of God in the Eucharist, I pointed out that His humility is a measure of His mercy. This needs more reflection in order to grasp the extent of His mercy given in the Eucharist. Here He reveals the extreme dimensions of His loving mercy, fully carrying out the Father's plan and will to perfection: *"God so loved the world that he gave his only Son"* (John 3:16). And so Jesus gave Himself completely.

The Eucharist is total gift, a complete giving to the extreme extent of His love, the ultimate gift of His mercy. Again we can consider His mercy given in three dimensions: given as presence, given as sacrifice, and given as communion.

The Eucharist is God's love given as Mercy Incarnate, mercy itself dwelling among us: **mercy present**, in the totality of His Body and Blood, Soul and Divinity—hidden, silent, humble, loving—to be adored and worshipped; **mercy sacrificed**, Body broken and given, Blood poured out for the forgiveness of sins in a new and everlasting covenant of merciful love—to be offered continually in remembrance of His passion, death and resurrection along with all our sacrifices, sufferings, joys; and, **mercy to be consumed** in Holy Communion, in an intimate union of Bride and Bridegroom that all may be one (John 17:21)—that we may be transformed into what we eat, that we may be truly loved and love in return.

This is God's gift of mercy, so completely given that He wants to be consumed by His faithful disciples so that we may be

9

one with Him as He is with the Father. There is no greater love given, no greater mercy poured out, than in the gift of one's very life.

Pope John Paul II, in his encyclical *Rich in Mercy* (#13), describes this mercy as "the most stupendous attribute of the Creator and of the Redeemer". He goes on to say that the Church brings us even nearer to the source of the Savior's mercy, especially in the Eucharist which brings us even nearer to that love which is more powerful than death: "For as often as we eat this bread and drink this cup, we proclaim not only the death of the Redeemer but also His resurrection, 'until He comes' in glory" (I Cor 11:26 and acclamation of the Roman Rite). He then points out that the celebration of the Eucharist attests to His inexhaustible love by which "He desires always to be united with us and present in our midst, coming to meet every human heart."

In every Mass and before every tabernacle, we proclaim this ultimate mercy of God, mercy revealed as the love of presence, of sacrifice, of union.

This is the merciful God that dwells in your hearts at this moment. Open wide the doors of your hearts and acknowledge His loving presence, with thanks and praise and rejoicing!

In Jesus our Merciful
Savior and Lord,
Father George

V. EUCHARIST AS PRESENCE

March 1, 1990

Dear Donna and Vinny,

May the merciful and Eucharistic Heart of Jesus reveal His loving presence to you in a new and profound way.

The presence of the Lord is special. Webster's dictionary has a long list of meanings for the word "presence" and "present". Here I am using the word for a real and unique "being here and now", in a particular place and time in the sense of our Lord Jesus Christ. Jesus is present in the Church and in our hearts by the Holy Spirit in a variety of ways:

> *The Spirit dwells in the Church and in the hearts of the faithful as in a temple.*
> (cf. I Cor 3:16; 6:19; *Lumen Gentium*, #4).

The Second Vatican Council also describes the presence of Christ in His Church in her liturgical celebrations: "He is present in the sacrifice of the Mass, not only in the person of His minister . . . but especially under the Eucharistic species." The Council Fathers go on to teach that Christ is present by His power in the Sacraments, present in His Word proclaimed in the Church, and present when the Church sings and prays (*Sacrosanctum Concilium* #7).

The **presence** of the Lord is the foundation of the three-fold dimension of the Eucharist giving "this truly most holy Sacrament its full magnitude and its essential meaning" according to John Paul II, who continues:

> *It is at one and the same time a sacrifice/Sacrament, a communion/Sacrament, and a presence/Sacrament*
> (*Redemptor Hominis*, #20).

11

In his letter to bishops and priests on the occasion of Holy Thursday, 1980, Pope John Paul II wrote of the close link between the Eucharistic liturgy and its sacredness:

> *It is a holy and sacred action because in it are the continual presence and action of Christ, "the Holy One" of God (Lk 1:34; Jn 6:69; Acts 3:14; Rev 3:7), "anointed by the Holy Spirit" (Acts 10:38; Lk 4:18), "consecrated by the Father" (Jn 10:36) to lay down his life of his own accord and to take it up again (Jn 10:17), and the High Priest of the new covenant (Heb 3:1; 4:15).*
>
> (*Dominicae Canae* #8)

Jesus Christ is continually present through the Holy Spirit and continues to accomplish His saving work as High Priest. At the celebration of the Eucharist, Jesus Christ's sacrificial offering of His life, death and resurrection is made present, present in order that we unite ourselves with this sacrifice (*Lumen Gentium*, #11; *Sacrosanctum Concilium*, #48; *Presbyterorum ordinis*, #4). The sacrifice of Christ is made present to us by the power of the Holy Spirit and the priestly words of institution of the Eucharist. What is made present before us here and now is the Body and Blood, Soul and Divinity of the Lord Jesus Christ as He is now—sacrificed, risen and glorified. This is the teaching of the Church.

This sacramental, sacrificial presence of the Lord Jesus Christ is what we receive in **Holy Communion**. Wonder of wonders, the almighty God humbles Himself totally to be consumed by us, present to us, in order to transform us into His presence in the world!

During my time in the hermitage in 1985, I composed a litany of presence. Over the years I've used it with groups on retreat and I've prayed it with growing meaning. May your reflection on the "prayer of presence" deepen your awareness and experience of the Lord Jesus present in the Eucharist and in your heart.

Father George

JESUS, YOU ARE PRESENT:

The RESPONSE is: Jesus, You are present:

Jesus, You are here in the Eucharist—
As Son of the Father and Son of Mary (Creed)—
As at the Annunciation when You the Word were
   made flesh (Lk 1; Jn 1)—
By word and the Spirit (Jn 3)—
As Mercy Incarnate (John Paul II)—
Because you love us (Jn 13:11)—
As the Lamb of God (Jn 1:29)—
As totally given and poured out (Lk 22:19-20)—
As the new covenant (Jn 6:27; Lk 22:20)—
Body and Blood, Soul and Divinity (Council of Trent)—
As the memorial of Your passion, death and
   resurrection (Canon of Mass)—
As the remembrance of all you have done for us (I Cor 11:25)—
As the thanksgiving to the Father (Mt 26:27)—
As the sacrificial gift to the Father (Heb 10:10)—
As the promise of resurrection (see I Cor 11:30)—
To give us eternal life (Jn 6:51-58)—
To nourish us (Jn 6:54)—
As "My Lord and my God" (Jn 20:28)—
As the icon of the invisible God (Col 1:15)—
Though hidden like the Father—
As a pleasing aroma to the Father (see II Cor 2:15)—
As Priest, Prophet and King—
As the Holy One, the Humble One, the Merciful One—
In all past and future (*O Sacrum convivium*)—
As the pledge of your coming again (see I Cor 11:26)—
As the Bridegroom longing for communion (Lk 22:15)—
As the mystery of faith—
As the mystery of mercy—
As the hope of glory—
Jesus, you are here and you call us (Jn 11:28)—

(*Icons of Mercy*, Faith Publishing Co.,
P.O. Box 237, Milford, OH 45150)

VI. EUCHARIST AS SACRIFICE

Dear Donna and Vinny,

May the merciful Lord strengthen you in your times of trials and testings.

The Lord Jesus came among us to share in all our miseries and humanity. By His love, He transformed suffering into sacrifice, bringing salvation to all of us. Now He invites you and me to unite our sufferings with His, with even the little love we can muster up, to be a sacrifice bringing His salvation to those in need. He invites all of us to be partners in His continued work of redemption.

The most effective way we can unite our sufferings with the sacrifice of Christ is through the Eucharist, which Christ left us, to remain with us. Church teaching has been consistent that the Eucharist is a sacrifice and we are to offer ourselves along with the Immaculate Victim:

> At the Last Supper, on the night when He was betrayed, our Savior instituted the **Eucharistic Sacrifice** of His Body and Blood. He did this in order to perpetuate the sacrifice of the Cross throughout the centuries until He should come again, and so to entrust to His beloved spouse, the Church, a memorial of His death and resurrection . . .
>
> Christ's faithful should be instructed by God's word and be refreshed at the table of the Lord's Body; they should give thanks to God; by offering the Immaculate Victim, not only through the hands of the priest, but also with him, they should learn to offer themselves too . . .
>
> (*Sacrosanctum Concilium*, #47, 48)

The teaching about offering our own selves along with the

14

Immaculate Victim is made even more explicit in the main document of Vatican II, the Dogmatic Constitution on the Church, which spells out the many aspects of our lives we should offer, exercising our baptismal priesthood:

> [As for the lay faithful,] . . . *all their works, prayers, and apostolic endeavors, their ordinary married and family life, their daily labor, their mental and physical relaxation, if carried out in the Spirit, and even the hardships of life, if patiently borne—all of these become spiritual sacrifices acceptable to God through Christ Jesus (see I Pt. 2:5). During the celebration of the Eucharist, these sacrifices are most lovingly offered to the Father along with the Lord's Body. Thus, as worshippers whose every deed is holy, laity consecrate the world itself to God.*
>
> (*Lumen Gentium*, #34).

The lay faithful "consecrate the world to the Father!" The people of God really are a priestly people. The ordained, ministerial priest consecrates the bread and wine to be the Body and Blood of Christ and the lay faithful, by means of the presence of the Eucharistic Body and Blood of Christ, now consecrate the world—and their lives, their families, their works and possessions. The lay faithful transform the world, that all may be divinized in Christ.

The lay faithful are charged with "living" the Eucharistic sacrifice so that Christ may be all in all. The Council Fathers conclude Section #48 of *Sacrosanctum Concilium*, quoted above, with this sweeping picture of the daily transformation of the world:

> *Through Christ the Mediator, [the Christian laity] should be drawn day by day into even closer union with God and with each other, so that finally God may be all in all.*   (*ibid.*, 48).

This means in practice that every one of our actions and desires, pains and joys, disappointments and hopes, loves and frustrations—all that we are, all that we do and think, all that we have—everything can be offered in —"spiritual sacrifice" in union with the Eucharist sacrifice for the sake of others.

Your pain and joy is precious, don't waste it! Offer it! Offer it for the members of your family, for families of the whole church and world in order that in Christ we may be one family, one Body of Christ to the glory of God the Father.

The making of "spiritual sacrifices" is always possible for us because the Eucharistic sacrifice is being offered continuously around the world. As an approximate calculation, consider that over 420,000 priests in the world offer over 300 Masses each per year—if calculated for the average number of Masses being offered at any given time (considering the Roman Mass lasts a half-hour), there are 8 to 10 thousand Masses being offered at this present moment around the world!

For from the rising of the sun, even to its setting, my name is great among the nations; and everywhere they bring sacrifice to my name and a pure offering.

(Mal 1:11)

A "spiritual sacrifice" is made by a simple and decisive act of the will: "I offer this _____ to you, Father, in union with the sacrifice of Jesus." Such an offering can be made even without words, or in the simplest words from the heart:

"Jesus, mercy!"

"Jesus, I trust in you!"

We can repeat this offering over and over again—each time the pain and the memory of the situation comes to mind. It seems that the Lord allows us to remember painful events and relationships so that we may continue to offer them up and so continue to transform the world. It may be good that we cannot forget some of the past hurts—because we remember to offer them. Of course, however, Our Lord wishes for us to work through such painful memories with forgiveness and love.

The offering of the pain as Eucharistic sacrifice with Christ doesn't take the pain away, but it surely gives it meaning and value.

A powerful Eucharistic offering was designed by Our Lord and taught to Sister Faustina Kowalska. He asked her to say it unceasingly: the "Chaplet of Divine Mercy". It is a Eucharistic offering that is available to all of us, at all times and places, to offer to the Eucharistic Lord. It is a continuation of the Mass. It is a "mini-Mass" as a brother priest, Father Sam Tiesi, T.O.R., at the Franciscan University of Steubenville told me. "I can't stop saying it!"

Christ told Sister Faustina that by praying in this way, her prayers would have great power for the conversion of sinners,

for peace for the dying, and even for controlling nature.
  We too can pray this chaplet:
    Using ordinary rosary beads of five decades, begin
    with the *Our Father*, *Hail Mary* and the *Creed*.

    Then, on the large beads we pray:
    "Eternal Father, I offer you the Body and Blood, Soul
    and Divinity of Your Dearly Beloved Son, Our Lord,
    Jesus Christ, in atonement for our sins and those of
    the whole world."

    On the small beads we pray:
    "For the sake of His sorrowful Passion, have mercy
    on us and on the whole world."

    And at the end, we pray three times:
    "Holy God, Holy Mighty One, Holy Immortal One,
    have mercy on us and on the whole world." (See
    Diary, 476).

                              In the Eucharistic Lord,
                              Father George

VII. EUCHARIST AS COMMUNION

February 3, 1990

Dear Donna and Vinny,

May the merciful Lord reveal His presence in your hearts. The Holy Eucharist is a communion with Christ in a very intimate way; it is a common-union-in-Christ. We consume His Body and Blood in order that we become what we eat and drink; that we become living Eucharist; that we may daily grow more fully into His mystical Body; that we may live His life:

> *He who feeds on my flesh and drinks my blood has eternal life . . .* (Jn 6:54)

The point I want to make is that this union with Christ is not only at the moment of reception of Holy Communion, but also this union can continue throughout our day:

> *Whoever eats my flesh and drinks my blood remains in me and I in him.* (Jn 6:56)

The Lord remains with us in our hearts as we live in Him and as He does in us.

Throughout the day, we can make "spiritual communions," uniting ourselves with His presence, living on in His love. A spiritual communion is an act of the will, an act of love uniting our hearts with His presence—a simple act, but a very loving and affectionate one.

St. Peter puts it this way: *Venerate the Lord, that is, Christ in your hearts* (I Pt. 3:15). St. Paul describes that union with Christ as "The mystery of Christ in you, your hope of glory" (Col 1:27).

For me, the practice of spiritual communion matured during my time of solitude with the Camaldolese Hermits. The lesson I carried away and have treasured ever since my first stay of three months was a message I felt in my heart:

To please me, be present to me with your heart . . . in
the heart of Mary, trusting, rejoicing.

To be present to the Lord with my heart is what pleases Him.
It is a loving, trusting and joyful awareness of His presence
in my heart. It is not analyzed, nor probed, but a silent presence.
It is a fire of divine love that we pray for in the Church's prayer
to the Holy Spirit:
"Come, Holy Spirit, fill the hearts of your faithful,
enkindle in them the fire of your divine love."

It is that fire of divine love that *"God has poured out into our
hearts through the Holy Spirit who has been given to us"* (Rom 5:5).

In Holy Communion and in spiritual communion, the Lord
speaks to us clearly and even loudly, but His language is silence!
We can commune so much in silent communion of love with
the Lord. Let your heart just love Him and let it remain in that
love. Let your heart be silent in His silent presence. Let your
heart glow with love for Him.
You know that the Lord is always present to us, but we are
not always present to Him. In His extreme humility He will
not force Himself upon us; instead, as described in the Book
of Revelation, He stands at the door of our hearts and knocks
and waits:
*Here I stand, knocking at the door. If anyone hears me
calling and opens the door, I will enter his house and have
supper with him, and he with me.* (Rev 3:20)

The Lord never refuses an invitation! If we ask Him to come
in, He will come in and share the heavenly banquet with us.
And more than that, as the text goes on to say:
*I will give the victor the right to sit with me on my throne,
as I myself won the victory and took my seat beside my
Father on his throne.* (Rev 3:21)

Holy Communion is a sharing in both the eternal banquet
and the throne of victory. It really is a common-union-in-Christ.
Holy Communion is also a proclamation of the death,
resurrection and coming again of the Lord. In the Eucharistic
prayer of the Mass our response to the priest's invitation, "Let
us proclaim the mystery of faith", is:

> *When we eat this bread and drink this cup, we proclaim*
> *your death, Lord Jesus, until you come in glory.*
>   (*Roman Liturgy, Acclamation* C)

Each time we celebrate Mass and receive Holy Communion we not only proclaim His coming again, but we also hasten the day of His coming by our devotion and holy conduct.

Let us receive the Lord in Holy Communion often and continue to venerate Him in our hearts by our spiritual communions, and so hasten the Day of His Coming!

> In Jesus the Eucharistic
> and merciful Lord,
> Father George

VIII. THE ACTION OF THE MASS

February 16, 1990

Dear Donna and Vinny,

"I attended Mass today."

These usual words describing our presence at Mass can reveal our attitude toward it. The phrase "I attended" implies a passive presence, a spectator presence. Such other phrases as "I went to Mass" or "I was at Mass", indicate a fundamental attitude that the Mass is something the priest does by himself.

Despite the teaching of Vatican II and the changes in the liturgy, both intended to increase **active** participation in the Mass, our language hasn't changed much. Does that indicate that our attitude hasn't changed much either?

As a priest, I consecrate the bread and wine to be the Body and Blood of Christ by the power of the Holy Spirit and the words of institution, through the power of Holy Orders. Yes, my role is to confect the Eucharist, to make the Lord present in a new sacramental way on this altar, at this time. But it is the role of **all** of the people of God, by the power of Baptism, to be active in the action of the Mass.

What action? What verbs describe the action of the Christian faithful at Mass? I would suggest three verbs that may sound presumptuous or ostentatious but really do identify the action of all of us at Mass.

These three verbs of action are taken from the text of the Eucharistic prayers of the Mass:

> **We proclaim...**
> **We offer...**
> **We celebrate...**

"We proclaim." As celebrant, I invite you to proclaim the mystery of our faith, immediately after the words of

21

consecration. We proclaim the presence of the Lord Jesus Christ who died but now is risen:

> When we eat this bread and drink this cup, we proclaim
> your death, Lord Jesus, until you come in glory.
>
> (Roman Liturgy, Acclamation C)

We, all of us together, priest and people, proclaim the presence of the Lord Jesus. Along with His death and resurrection, we proclaim and profess our own dying with Him in order to rise with Him.

"To proclaim" is an action that describes what we do at Mass. *"Today at Mass I proclaimed the death and resurrection of the Lord Jesus Christ and His coming again!"* Now that would be a marvellous way to express our "attendance" at Mass!

"We offer." We offer the oblation, the sacrifice of Christ Jesus on the Cross. It is the same oblation that Jesus made on Holy Thursday night in offering His death on the Cross the next day. Now in remembrance of Him and what He did for us, *"We offer you (Father) in thanksgiving this holy and living sacrifice"* (Eucharistic Prayer #3). This is the prayer I (as a priest) say in the name of all of us after the proclamation of faith. But again it must be stressedthat it is all of us: **We offer** the Immaculate Victim along with our very lives. This offering of the very sacrifice of Christ is done in thanksgiving for His ultimate gift of mercy and humility.

"We celebrate." Use of the word "celebrate" to describe what happens at Mass is somewhat more common. As a priest, I usually have said, "I celebrated Mass", but that is not an expression the laity would commonly use to describe their own participation in the Mass. Shouldn't the lay faithful also experience and express their part in the Mass as a celebration, as in "We celebrated Mass with Father N.?"

The word "celebrate" is used in the first Eucharistic prayer following the proclamation of faith:

> Father, we celebrate the memory of Christ, Your Son. We,
> your people and your ministers recall His passion, His
> death and resurrection from the dead and His ascension
> into glory.

It is interesting to note how explicit the text is: **"We**, your people and your ministers" **celebrate**.

The word celebration can also refer to Holy Communion. We truly do celebrate a "common-union-in-Christ". Prior to

Communion, as celebrant of the Mass, I lift up the consecrated Host before the people and say:

This is the Lamb of God who takes away the sins of the world. Happy are they who are called to His supper.

(Roman Liturgy)

"Happy are they who" **celebrate** this ultimate gift of the Lord. How could I ever be worthy? We respond in words that reflect the humility of the centurion (see Lk 7:6) in proclaiming:

Lord I am not worthy to receive you, but only say the word and I shall be healed.

I would propose that we consciously try to express our role in the Mass using these active verbs:

We proclaim the presence of the Lord at Mass.
We offer the oblation of Christ Jesus at Mass.
We celebrate communion with Christ at Mass.

These active verbs may seem awkward at first, but they will mature and can become a meaningful part of our vocabulary and an accurate way to describe what we did when we "went to Mass".

Could this kind of active expression be of help to our teenagers, who complain: "I don't get anything out of Mass."? Can they be taught to ask instead: "Have I **proclaimed** the Lord's presence? Have I **offered** His sacrifice? Have I **celebrated** communion with Him and with others?"

In the Eucharistic Lord,
Father George

IX. EUCHARIST: PREFIGURED IN THE OLD TESTAMENT

March 17, 1990

Dear Donna and Vinny,

The Eucharist, with its dimensions of presence, sacrifice, and communion, is symbolized for us in the Old Testament. There are a number of well-known symbolic events that look forward to the fullness of the Eucharist. Also, some not so well-known events were pointed out to me by Father Gerry Farrell, M.M., now working for perpetual Eucharistic adoration in parishes in Korea. He showed me that Elijah, the great prophet, acted out the three dimensions of the Eucharist.

The sacrificial dimension is seen in Elijah's showdown with the four hundred priests of Baal who couldn't call down their gods; Elijah invoked the living God, and fire came down and consumed his offering (I Kings 18:38). Then, during his escape after this event, an angel of the Lord brought him bread and water to strengthen him, so that he might be able to walk the forty days and nights to Mount Horeb (I Kings 19:5-8). Here on the mountain where Moses had received the Law, Elijah sat in a cave and waited for the presence of the Lord, which did not come in the mighty wind, nor in the earthquake, nor in the fire, but in a gentle breeze (I Kings 9:11-13). As you see, sacrifice, communion, and presence were prefigured in the life of this prophet, who later appeared to Jesus, along with Moses, on Mount Tabor during the Transfiguration (Lk 9:28-36).

Moses, the figure of the Law of the Old Testament, also prefigured the Eucharist. The sacrifice of the lamb, and the sprinkling of its blood on the doorposts of the Israelites, saved them from the angel of death (Ex 12:21-27). The manna, the bread from heaven, was their daily food in the desert (Ex 16:4). The presence of the Lord was manifested in the cloud of glory over the ark of the covenant and in the pillar of fire at night, as well as by the presence of the showbread before the ark of the Lord (Ex 25:30). Again, sacrifice, communion and presence foreshadow the fullness of God's presence with His people. These symbols from the Exodus of the Israelites are commonly used symbols of the Eucharist.

On the second Sunday of Lent, the Gospel which is read describes Jesus' transfiguration on Mount Tabor and the appearance of Moses and Elijah speaking with Him. The first reading on that same Sunday, taken from the Old Testament, delineates the Lord's covenant with Abraham whose history, like that of Moses and Elijah, also prefigures the three elements of the Eucharist: The priest Melchizedek offers bread and wine and blesses Abraham (Gen 14:18). Abraham is tested by the Lord's call to sacrifice his own son Isaac (Gen 22: 1-18). Abraham recognizes the presence of the Lord in the three angelic visitors, who appear to him as men, but who are the Lord and two of His messengers; Abraham feeds and welcomes them, and is afterwards blessed with an only son whom he later proves willing to sacrifice at the Lord's command (Gen 18:1-8). Once again, we find the three fundamental dimensions of the Eucharist—presence, sacrifice and communion.

I am especially impressed by the signs of the Lord's presence. Abraham's faith in the Lord gave him the sensitivity to recognize the presence of the Lord. The Lord's presence to His people in the desert was seen not only in the visible cloud and pillar of fire over the ark, but also in the silent presence of the showbread which the Lord commanded to be present before the ark: *"On the table you shall always keep showbread set before me"* (Ex 25:30). The bread is called "the bread of presence" or literally, "the bread of the face". This is a symbol that I have not seen developed as a Eucharistic symbol. The "tiny whispering sound", which Elijah heard as the presence of the Lord, made him hide his face in his cloak (I Kings 19:12-13).

How truly this "tiny whispering sound" is symbolic of the humble and hidden **presence** of Christ in the Eucharist. How true it is that we need to approach the Eucharist with faith and a quiet heart, to be aware of His radiant presence now cloaked beneath the appearance of bread and wine, instead of shining forth as a cloud of glory or pillar of fire.

The Old Testament symbols of **sacrifice** (Abraham offering his son, Moses sprinkling the blood of the lamb, and Elijah calling down fire from heaven on his offering) are a reminder that teaches us the power of the sacrifice of the Mass to cleanse us and the whole world of our sins.

The symbols of **communion** teach us the loving and transforming union with Him, that the Lord desires for us. We eat not just the bread and wine of Melchizedek, nor the manna provided in the desert, nor the bread and water that strengthened Elijah; rather, we commune with the Lord Himself. We are fed, nourished and transformed by the Body and Blood, Soul and Divinity of the Lord Jesus Christ—the Bread of Life.

The Lord has prepared us well for appreciating and participating in the Eucharistic **presence**, **sacrifice**, and **communion**.

In the Eucharistic Lord,
Father George

X. THE RADIANCE OF THE EUCHARIST

March 19, 1990

Dear Donna and Vinny,

Peace and joy be with you.

I would love to see the Eucharist radiate! It has been a desire of my heart for a number of years to have the Lord reign among us in resplendent glory. The radiant presence of the Lord in the Eucharist would be a marvelous sign of God's presence among us and an effective sign to evangelize. Could you imagine the surprise of a non-believer or a doubting Thomas entering into the Eucharistic presence and seeing the Lord's radiance, and being floored by His power like Saul on the road to Damascus.

Come, Lord Jesus!

At the present time, the Eucharist does radiate to be seen and felt by faith. The Lord, hidden in His humility, calls forth our trust and faith. As we spend time before the Eucharistic presence, we are irradiated; our trust and faith are enlightened, and our hearts inflamed with the fire of His divine love. It is something like sun-bathing, only here we are "Son-bathing." It really is "radiation therapy"!

A few years ago, at a time when I was dealing with tensions and exhaustion which were overwhelming me, I went to a retreat at Holy Trinity Retreat House in Larchmont, NY. There Father Kevin Scallon, C.M., and Sister Briege McKenna prayed over me for the Lord's direction in that situation. Sister Briege shared this word: "Rest on the Sacred Heart. Take much time before the Blessed Sacrament. In time He will reveal His will. Trust Him."

Over the past three years I have deliberately taken more and more time before the Blessed Sacrament. Currently, as I experiment with various prayer schedules to develop a realistic daily pattern for the Apostles of Divine Mercy, I am making three Holy Hours per day, one during the night, a second in the morning, and a third in the afternoon. The more time I spend before the exposed Blessed Sacrament, the more I desire to live in union with Him, to be a "living Eucharist" and to radiate His mercy, drawing strength from His merciful Heart in the Eucharist.

I am becoming more aware that His Eucharistic radiance is a radiance of mercy, a radiance of His Blood and Water that gushed forth from His pierced side on the Cross. Those are rays of mercy; the blood which is the life of the soul, and the water that justifies the soul, making it righteous. The red and pale rays which Sister Faustina saw radiating from the Heart of Jesus when He appeared to her, she also saw emanating from the Eucharist on a number of occasions (*Diary*, #370, 336, 344, 346, 657, 1462); at times she saw them radiating over the whole world (*Diary* #'s 420, 441, 1046):

> "Once the image [of the merciful Jesus] was being exhibited over the altar during the Corpus Christi procession [June 20, 1935]. When the priest exposed the Blessed Sacrament, and the choir began to sing, the rays from the image pierced the Sacred Host and spread out all over the world. Then I heard these words: "These rays of mercy will pass through you, just as they have passed through this Host, and they will go out through all the world." At these words, profound joy invaded my soul."   (*Diary*, #1046)

Shouldn't all the faithful be irradiated with His mercy in order that we may radiate His mercy to others? Then we would truly live the command of our Lord: *"Be merciful even as your Father is merciful"* (Lk 6:36).

I was excited when I read an account of the apparitions in Akita, Japan:

> "On June 12, 1973, when Sister Agnes Sasagawa, to whom Our Lady entrusted the messages, opened the tabernacle for adoration of the Blessed Sacrament, a very strong light came from it and filled the entire chapel. This lasted for three days."
> (Notes of Father Michael Scanlan, T.O.R.)

The Eucharist radiates! What a sign to the world if all could see it.

Father Stefano Gobbi records locutions from Mary speaking of the radiance of the Lord's coming reign. The locution of August 21, 1987, is especially clear and strong on the radiance of the Eucharist to come:

> "Because in the Eucharist Jesus Christ is really present, and this presence will become increasingly stronger, will shine over the earth like a sun and will mark the beginning of a new era. The coming of the glorious reign of Christ will coincide with the greatest splendor of the Eucharist. Christ will restore His glorious reign in the universal triumph of His Eucharistic reign which will unfold in all its power and will have the capacity to change hearts, souls, individuals, families, society and the very structure of the world."
>
> (*Our Lady Speaks to Her Beloved Priests*)

This radiant reign of the Eucharistic Lord is what I long for and pray for. Come, Lord Jesus! I realize that the glorious reign will come, but only after we have passed through the purification of a corporate Calvary. But if we keep our eyes fixed on Jesus, we, too, will endure the travail for the sake of the joy that lies ahead.

The radiant reign of Jesus is already prefigured for us in the event of Mt. Tabor, a preview of what is to come. Also, we are told of the radiance of the Lamb of God who will be the light of the New Jerusalem, replacing the sun and moon (see Rev 21:11; 22:5):

> *All of us, gazing on the Lord's glory with unveiled faces, are being transformed from glory to glory into his very image by the Lord who is the Spirit.* (II Cor 3:18)

In the radiance of the
Eucharistic Lord,
Father George

XI. A EUCHARISTIC PARABLE

March 20, 1990

Dear Donna and Vinny,

This is a spiritual-biochemical parable of the Eucharist! A spiritual-biochemical parable? Yes, a parable of multi-levels is needed to describe the transforming power of the Eucharist. The Eucharist transforms us from glory to glory each time we receive Holy Communion, or gaze upon its radiance (see II Cor 3:18).

Once upon a time the wheat in the field was given the gift of speech. It spoke to the soil, asking, "Soil, how would you like to become wheat?"

"What do you mean?" replied the soil.

"Well, you don't need to stay as dirt, you could become part of me, and grow and have kernels of grain with golden hair, and wave in the wind," said the wheat.

But immediately the soil inquired, "How can this happen?"

"Well," said the wheat, "just say 'Yes,' and when the rains come and dissolve some of your minerals I'll absorb you, draw you up into myself and you'll become part of me."

"Is it really true?" wondered the soil.

"Oh, what joy and beauty is in store for you!" promised the wheat. And so the soil said a humble "Yes". When the rains came and soaked the soil, the wheat roots reached out and drew the minerals up into the wheat, and the soil became part of the golden grain which grew and waved in the breeze under the summer sun.

Then one day a lamb jumped the fence into the field and said to the wheat, "Hey, wheat, how would you like to become a lamb?"

"What do you mean?" the wheat answered.

"Well, you wouldn't have to stay in one place, rooted in the soil. You could skip and jump, grow wool and make more lambs," explained the lamb.

"But, oh, what will it cost me?" said the wheat.

"It will cost you a total 'yes', a surrender to me, and then I will eat you up, digest and absorb you and then you will be part of me."

"Is it worth it?" asked the wheat, trembling in the wind.

"Oh, you have no idea what it is to be a lamb! Come now and say 'Yes'!"

And so the wheat tipped its head of grain and said a quiet "yes". The lamb ate the wheat, digested it, absorbed it, and the wheat became part of the lamb, which bounded across the field and joyfully skipped back over the fence into the pasture.

Then the lamb heard the voice of the shepherd. "Hey, lamb, how would you like to become part of me?" A chill ran down the spine of the lamb as it bleated. "That sounds like the question I just asked the wheat!"

"Oh yes, it may be similar, but what a difference!" You have no idea what it is to be a man! You could love and think, choose and create, invent and write, and more!"

The lamb was curious about this new kind of life and really wanted something more, so despite his fear, he meekly bowed his head and said, "Yes." The shepherd sacrificed the lamb, cut him up, roasted him and had a fine meal.

After his meal, the shepherd was walking in his garden in the cool of the evening and he heard the voice of God. "Hey, man, how would you like to become a son of God?" On hearing the voice of God, the man hid himself for fear, but God pursued him and again asked, "How would you like to be like me?"

Trembling, the man responded, "I am afraid of what it will cost me. I know what it cost the lamb that I had for supper."

"Do not be afraid, oh man," said God reassuringly, "I had My Son pay the cost for you. He has shown the way to Me, step by step. He became man. Then the shepherd that laid down His life for His sheep, buried in the ground like grain to bring forth new life as the living bread, a lamb pierced yet risen and victorious, wants to bathe you in His life-giving blood that you may be transformed, transfigured, divinized!

"You will become sons and daughters of God, members of the body of My beloved Son, if you say, 'Yes' and surrender to My will and plan for you. Unless you eat the flesh of My Son and drink His blood you will not have life in you. When you do eat His flesh and drink His blood, you will become what you eat and drink, and have eternal life. You will become sons and daughters of God."

Some men heard this proposal of God and couldn't accept it, and so walked away sad and confused. Others heard this proposal and their hearts began to be warmed with expectation and they asked, "Is it really true?"

And God said, "What no eye has seen, nor ear heard, nor the heart of man conceived, I have prepared for those who love Me, and this I have revealed through My Spirit" (see I Cor 2:9-10).

And so, for those whose hearts were burning within them, for those who said, "Yes" to God's proposal and plan, it began to happen. Day by day, year by year, the transformation took place and they began to radiate His mercy to the world.

This spiritual-biochemical parable of transformation is true. Besides, it is good biochemistry. We really do become what we eat!

In the Eucharistic Lord,
Father George

XII. MARY, MOTHER OF THE EUCHARIST

March 21, 1990

Dear Donna and Vinny,

As the solemnity of the Annunciation of our Lord's conception in the womb of Mary approaches, my thoughts have been on the role of Mary in the Incarnation and the Eucharist.

Mary's response to the Angel Gabriel's announcement of the plan of the Lord was:

> Behold, I am the handmaid of the Lord: Let it be done
> to me according to your word.   (Lk 1:38)

Mary said "Yes" to the plan of God and "the Word was made flesh and dwelt among us" (Jn 1:14) by the power of the Holy Spirit. Jesus also said "Yes" to the plan of the Father:

> When he came into the world, he said, "Sacrifices and
> offerings you did not desire, but a body you prepared for
> me; in burnt offerings and sin offerings you have taken
> no pleasure. Then I said, 'Behold, I have come to do your
> will, O God, and it is written of me in the roll of the
> book.'"   (Heb 10:5-8)

By saying "Yes" to the will of the Father, Mary, Jesus, and the Holy Spirit cooperated with the will and plan of the Father, and **we** by that will, have been sanctified through the offering of the body of Jesus Christ once for all (Heb 10:10). We have been sanctified by the body of Jesus Christ and by our "Yes" to the will of the Father.

Our willed "Yes" to the will of the Father continues as we say "Yes" to the cooperative action of Mary, Jesus, and the Holy

33

Spirit, thereby becoming the living, mystical Body of Christ, being transformed into "living Eucharist". "How can this be . . . ?" we ask, echoing the words of Mary. *"The Holy Spirit will come upon you"* (Lk 1:35), was the response, just as the celebrant of the Mass invokes the Holy Spirit upon the faithful:

> *Grant that we who are nourished by His body and blood*
> *may be filled with His Holy Spirit and become one body,*
> *one spirit in Christ.*

(Third Eucharistic Prayer, Roman Rite)

The Second Vatican Council teaches that "the faithful, already marked with the sacred seal of baptism and confirmation, are through the reception of the Eucharist, fully joined to the Body of Christ" (*Decree on the Ministry and Life of Priests*, #5).

How are we prepared for this full union, to be "fully joined to the Body of Christ"? I see this as Mary's role. We allow her to fulfill her role in the Father's plan of salvation, by our willed "Yes" to her. This is what consecration to Mary means. It allows her to bring us to the cross of Jesus, to incorporate us into His one sacrifice, in order that we become the Body of Christ, living Eucharist.

The dying words of Jesus are Eucharistic. By saying to Mary, *"Woman, behold your son"*, and to the disciple, *"Behold your mother"*, Jesus is telling His mother and the disciple whom He loves, who represents each of us, that we are now, like Jesus, children of the Mother of God and therefore, members of His Body—living Eucharist. He then *"gave up his spirit"* (Jn 19:30), and it was accomplished.

The Gospel of St. John does not record the words of institution of the Eucharist as such, but John does give us the discourse of Jesus on the Eucharist (Jn 6:25-70), as well as Jesus' description of the effects of the Eucharist, at the Last Supper (Jn 14-17). In his mystical way, John does give us a deeper meaning of the words of institution of the Eucharist, however, in the dying words of Jesus from the Cross: "Woman, behold your son" (Jn 19:26). In a profoundly mystical sense, Jesus was pronouncing the words of institution over us ("This is My Body"), by also making us children of Mary. We are His body, and so we become living Eucharist, sons and daughters of the Mother of God. Through consecration to Mary, we allow her to prepare the living bread, to prepare us to live a total "Yes" and to be this living Eucharist, the Body of Christ.

So we, too, say, "Behold the handmaid of the Lord," and since God provided a body for us, we say as well, "I have come to do your will", and we "offer our bodies as a living sacrifice, holy and acceptable to God" (see Rom 12:1). So, as a priestly people we "take part in the Eucharistic sacrifice, which is the fount and apex of the whole Christian life, and offer the divine victim to God, and offer ourselves along with it" (*Lumen Gentium*, #11).

Throughout each day, we can continue to offer the divine victim and ourselves as well, in the Eucharistic words of Jesus, and of Mary at the Annunciation:

Behold the handmaid of the Lord. Be it done unto me according to your word.

or

(Behold, you have provided a body for me . . . I have come to do your will.)

We can offer ourselves, our families , others, the world situation, everything, in words that echo the Eucharistic proclamation of John the Baptist:

Behold, the lamb of God, who takes away the sin of the world!   (Jn 1:30)

When we see the brokenness of the Body of Christ around us, we can cry to the Father:

"Behold, the pierced lamb of God, and have mercy on us and on the whole world!"

At each occasion of pain, we can cry to the Father:

"Behold, the broken Body of Your Son, and have mercy on us and on the whole world."

We can live the Mass from moment to moment as we live our "Yes" to be living Eucharist—chosen, blessed, and broken, to be given for the sake of the many.

> In Jesus, our Eucharistic Lord,
> and in Mary, Mother of
> the Eucharist,
> Father George

XIII. AN EXAMPLE OF LIVING EUCHARIST

March 29, 1990

Dear Donna and Vinny,

May the Lord bless you with a deeper life in the Eucharist.

A very special example of being a living Eucharist is Sister Faustina Kowalska. Her full name gives us this message: Sister Maria Faustina of the Blessed Sacrament. Her example in living a Eucharistic life shows us how the Eucharist is the answer to the crisis in the Church and world.

She makes a revealing statement about her life and the significance of the Eucharist:

"The most solemn moment of my life is the moment when I receive Holy Communion. I long for each Holy Communion, and every Holy Communion, I give thanks to the most Holy Trinity."

(*Diary*, #1804)

Her Eucharistic life centered on the three dimensions we have written about and used as a foundation to explain the full meaning of the Eucharist: Eucharist as presence, sacrifice, and communion.

Eucharist as Presence

Sister Faustina was very aware of the presence of the Lord Jesus in the Eucharist. How often she would come to adore Him present in the tabernacle and spend hours of worship and intercession for souls in need.

A regular experience for her was the vision of the Lord in the Eucharist at Mass and at Benediction. Over sixty such visions are recorded in her *Diary*, most of them involving the child Jesus, on a few occasions the Holy Infant with His blessed

Mother. At other times the vision vouch-safed as she adored the Host, was that of Jesus during His passion, and sometimes of Him in His majesty.

Some dozen times she records seeing the rays of mercy emanating from the Holy Eucharist, as depicted in the image of the merciful Savior; at times these rays extended themselves in her vision until they covered the world. What a powerful message of the Eucharist radiating out on the world! We need this radiation therapy!

A special gift given to Sister Faustina was the continuous presence of the Eucharist within her from the time of one Holy Communion until the next. During midnight Mass, 1935, after Holy Communion she heard these words:

> "I am always in your heart, not only when you receive Me in Holy Communion but always."
>
> *(Diary, #575)*

She was aware of this gift:

> "I have come to know that Holy Communion remains in me until the next Holy Communion."
>
> *(Diary, #1302)*

Throughout the day she adored Jesus present and asked for graces, especially for children.　　　　*(Diary, #1821)*

Eucharist as Sacrifice

Sister Faustina was given a vision of the institution of the Holy Eucharist on a Holy Thursday in the Cenacle. She came to understand that the essence of the sacrifice was in Christ's offering of Himself on the night before He died: "the essence is in the Cenacle" *(Diary, #684, 757, 832)*.

She expressed the depth of this mystery as a "miracle of mercy" and prayed that the whole world would come to know this unfathomable mercy.

> "What awesome mysteries take place during Mass! . . . One day we will know what God is doing for us in each Mass and what sort of gift He is preparing in it for us."　　　　*(Diary, #914)*

A very special aspect of Sister's life was her desire to be transformed into a living host, a wafer, hidden and broken, to be given to others:

"Jesus, transform me, miserable and sinful as I am, into Your own self (for You can do all things), and give me to Your Eternal Father. I want to be a sacrificial host before You, but an ordinary wafer to people. I want the fragrance of my sacrifice to be known to You alone."   (*Diary*, #483)

"Transform me into Yourself, O Jesus, that I may be a living sacrifice and pleasing to You. I desire to atone at each moment for poor sinners."
                                                    (*Diary*, #908)

Jesus answered her prayers, telling her: *"You are a living host, pleasing to the Heavenly Father"* (*Diary*, #932, 1826). Sister Faustina felt this transformation as a holy fire, present in her always:
All the good that is in me is due to Holy Communion. I owe everything to it. I feel that this holy fire has transformed me completely. Oh, how happy I am to be a dwelling for You, O Lord! My heart is a temple in which You dwell continually.
                                                    (*Diary*, #1392)

She truly lived the reality of the prayer: "Come, Holy Spirit, fill the hearts of the faithful and enkindle in them the fire of Your divine love."
The experience of being a "Living host", hidden, broken, and given was the central experience of her life—but, this experience was based on the union of love with the living God.

Eucharist as Communion
Sister Faustina experienced union with the Lord most profoundly in conjunction with the Holy Eucharist, either during Mass and Holy Communion, or during adoration of the Blessed Sacrament. The Lord described her union with Him as being like that of a bride:
"Here, I am entirely yours, soul, body, and divinity, as your Bridegroom. You know what love demands: one thing only, reciprocity . . ."   (*Diary*, #1770)

As a bride she prepared for Holy Communion:
"I am preparing myself for Your coming as a bride

does for her bridegroom."   (*Diary*, #1805)

At times during Holy Communion she experienced a union with the Holy Trinity:
> "At that moment, I was drawn into the bosom of the most Holy Trinity, and I was immersed in the love of the Father, the Son and the Holy Spirit. These moments are hard to describe."   (*Diary*, #1670)

These times of union are a "mystery of love" in the words of the Lord Jesus (*Diary*, #156) and a taste of eternity.

Holy Communion was the strength and support of Sister Faustina in her day's struggle. The Lord taught her: "In the host is your power; it will defend you" (*Diary*, #616). She added that the Eucharist was her strength, even in her tender years:
> "Once, when I was seven years old, at a vespers service, conducted before the Lord Jesus in the monstrance, the love of God was imparted to me for the first time and filled my little heart; and the Lord gave me understanding of divine things."
>   (*Diary*, #1404)

Throughout her *Diary* she constantly recorded the strength she received from the Eucharist.

The Eucharist as the Answer

The Eucharist was the answer Sister Faustina needed and wanted for her life in Christ and her mission. The Eucharist is also the answer for our needs in this time of crisis in the Church and world. The lessons our Lord taught Sister Faustina through the Eucharist are also intended for each of us, and available to each of us.

The Holy Eucharist was a precious time of teaching for Sister Faustina by Our Lord Jesus: teaching about her mission of winning souls, the way to live a spiritual life by abiding in Him, His desire to give graces in the Eucharist, praying in union with Mary, and offering to the Father the Blood and wounds of Jesus in the Mass as an act of expiation for sins. These teachings are the great mystery of the institution of the Holy Eucharist. The Lord used the occasion of Holy Communion as a time of profound teaching, and He desires to do the same for us.

The special place of the Holy Eucharist in the life of Sister Faustina can be summed up both in her full official name, Sister Maria Faustina of the Blessed Sacrament, and in the name she called herself after her oblation: "My name is to be 'sacrifice'" (*Diary*, #135). The Lord Jesus summed up her life in what He called her: "You are a living host" (*Diary*, #1826).

Her greatest desire was to be Eucharist, hidden like Jesus, blessed by her union with the Lord, broken like Jesus in the passion and totally given for the salvation of souls. Her prayer to be consecrated sums up her life:

"I am a white host before You, O Divine Priest. Consecrate me Yourself, and may my transubstantiation be known only to You. I stand before You each day as a sacrificial host and implore Your mercy upon the whole world."   (*Diary*, #1564)

For Sister Faustina of the Blessed Sacrament, the Eucharist was the answer to crisis in the Church, and in the world, and it is the answer for us now! It is Christ's "miracle of mercy".

In the victorious and Eucharistic Lord Jesus, Father George

XIV. THE HOLY EUCHARIST

January 4, 1991

Dear Donna and Vinny,

Eleven months have gone by since I started writing these letters on the Eucharist. After "proclaiming, offering, and celebrating" Mass and after a time of Eucharistic adoration, I just re-read the letters on Eucharist written last Lent. The gestation period has been fruitful. I now want to bring my reflections to a conclusion by considering the Eucharist as **Holy** and then as **Spiritual Energy**.

During my vigil Holy Hour this past night, a flash of insight on the Eucharist as "holy" filled my heart and mind. The holiness of the Eucharist is in the third dimension of the Eucharist which I described earlier as the ultimate humility and ultimate mercy of the Lord. The Eucharist is the holy-humble-merciful presence of the Lord Jesus. This third dimension completes the trilogy of descriptions with His mystery—God's total transcendence and holiness. This holy God emptied Himself in utter humility and mercy to be present among us by His Holy Spirit.

This holiness of God is proclaimed in every celebration of the Eucharist:

Holy, holy, holy Lord, God of power and might,
heaven and earth are full of your glory.
Hosanna in the highest.
Blessed is He who comes in the name of the Lord.
Hosanna in the highest.

After this proclamation, the priest continues in the (Second) Eucharistic prayer:

Lord, you are holy indeed,
the fountain of all holiness.
Let your Spirit come upon these gifts
to make them holy,

41

so that they may become for us
the body and blood of our Lord, Jesus Christ.

At each celebration of the Divine Liturgy of the Byzantine Rite, the priest proclaims at the elevation of the holy bread:
"Holy things for the Holy,"
and the people respond:
"One is Holy, one is Lord,
Jesus Christ,
to the glory of God the Father, Amen."
(The Liturgy of St. John Chrysostum)

In this liturgy, how powerfully the Trisagion (thrice-holy hymn) is sung prior to the reading of Sacred Scripture:
"Holy God! Holy Mighty One!
Holy Immortal One!
Have mercy on us!"
(The Liturgy of St. John Chrysostum)

This holiness of the Eucharist—the living, holy Lord present to us—calls for our reverence and awe, a holy fear of God, Who is not only so holy, but so totally humble and merciful. This holiness of the Eucharist is the third dimension of the counter-sign to the people of our age who have lost their sense of reverence, and of the holy.

The holiness of the Eucharist is the work of the Holy Spirit. This same Holy Spirit overshadowed Mary at the Annunciation, and Jesus, the Holy One, was conceived. It is this same Holy Spirit Who transforms bread and wine into the Body and Blood of Christ. It is the same Holy Spirit Who will transform us into living Eucharist, radiating His mercy as we continue our "Yes" to the Father in union with the "Yes" of Jesus and Mary.

This third dimension of the Eucharist reflects the nature of Christ's priesthood in which we all share by our Baptism, and some by Holy Orders. Expressed in terms of the Lord's command, echoing Sacred Scripture, we are called to:
"Be holy, because I am holy.
Be humble, because I am humble.
Be merciful, because I am merciful."

This three-fold dimension of the Eucharist, as the "holy-humble-merciful" presence of the Lord Jesus, also reflects the fundamental three-fold description of the Sacrament of presence/sacrifice/communion. As we are challenged to live out the Mass by "spiritual" presence, sacrifice and communion, so, too, we are challenged to be holy, humble, and merciful.

The Holy Eucharist is a challenge for you and me, and for all believers, to be and live the Eucharist—to be living Eucharist and so radiate the Lord's mercy on the whole world.

Come, Holy Spirit, transform me to be living Eucharist. Make my heart radiate with Your mercy. In union with Mary, Your beloved spouse, make my heart the throne of Jesus in His glorious coming.

Come, Lord Jesus!
Father George

XV. THE SPIRITUAL ENERGY
OF EUCHARIST

January 15, 1991

Dear Donna and Vinny,

May the Lord fill you with His radiant presence.

I've been searching for a "spiritual-biochemical" equation for the Eucharist. Of course, I'm aware that you can't describe the Eucharist by an equation, but I've had an inner urge to keep searching for an equation that would help describe the various dimensions of the Eucharist, and help us to remember them. This week, in prayer, I've come up with an equation for the spiritual energy of the Eucharist! It has been an exciting insight for me and so I want to share it.

As you may know, the great equation for physical energy was the product of the insight of Albert Einstein. He proposed that energy and matter are interconvertible, and when matter is converted into energy, there is a tremendous release of energy. He described this conversion in the simple equation:

$$e = mc^2$$

That is, energy (e) is equal to the mass of matter (m), multiplied by the speed of light (c) twice. His theoretical equation was proved to be correct in the first explosion of an atomic bomb: matter was converted into explosive energy! This is physical energy.

Is there a spiritual energy?

In regard to God's omnipotence, St. Thomas Aquinas said that the mercy of God: "forgiving men, taking pity on them, is a greater work than the creation of the world" (*Suma Theologiae*, Treatise on Grace, II-II. 113.9). He is saying that God's spiritual energy is greater than His physical energy of creation. So the search for an equation of spiritual energy became even more significant for me.

And Eureka, I think I've found such an equation! It describes the conversion of God's mercy into the radiant energy of the Eucharist:

$$E = mh^2$$

That is, the spiritual energy of the Eucharist (E) is equal to God's mercy (m), multiplied by His humility (h), and multiplied a second time by His holiness (h).

God's spiritual energy is greater than His physical energy expressed in creation. God's spiritual energy is given to us in the holy, humble, merciful presence of the Eucharist.

It radiates spiritual energy!

I would refer you back to the reflection on the "Radiance of the Eucharist". The source of the radiant spiritual energy is God's mercy transformed by His holiness and humility. It comes forth from the Eucharist as rays of mercy.

Recall how Sister Faustina Kowalska saw the Eucharist radiate with the same red and pale rays as in the image representing the Blood and water that gushed forth from the pierced Heart of Jesus. At times she saw these rays radiate out upon the whole world. (*Diary*, #420, 441, 1046).

This is radiant spiritual energy. We need to be irradiated by these rays of mercy, by His precious Blood and the water which gushed forth from His pierced, merciful Heart as a fount of mercy for us. We need to take extended time before the Eucharist for "Radiation Therapy". We need to be irradiated by His mercy, so that we may in turn radiate His mercy to the world.

> "O Blood and water which gushed forth from the Heart of Jesus as a fount of mercy for us, I trust in you."   (*Diary*, #309)

Another way that we can be transformed by the spiritual energy of the Eucharist is by "gazing" upon the radiant presence of the Lord. This gazing is perceiving with the eyes of faith, the true spiritual beauty before us. Again it is good to remind ourselves of the words of St. Paul:

> *All of us, gazing on the Lord's glory with unveiled faces, are being transformed from glory to glory into his very image by the Lord who is the Spirit.* (II Cor 3:18)

As we gaze upon the Eucharist with eyes of faith, with

"unveiled faces", we are gradually transformed into what we see—a living Eucharist, holy, humble, and merciful.

The great moment of transformation takes place when we receive the Eucharist, this spiritual radiant energy, in Holy Communion. We receive the Body and Blood, Soul and Divinity of the Lord Jesus Christ under the appearance of bread and wine, but transformed by the Holy Spirit. It is the same Holy Spirit that came upon Mary; it is the same Holy Spirit that came upon Jesus in the Jordan River; it is the same Holy Spirit by which Jesus performed the works of the Father and by which Jesus was resurrected; it is the same Holy Spirit that came upon the disciples in the Cenacle on Pentecost, transforming them, and the Church was born.

It is this same Holy Spirit that the priest asks to transform us into living Eucharist:

> Grant that we, who are nourished by His body and blood,
> may be filled with his Holy Spirit, and become one body,
> one spirit in Christ.
> 　　　　　　　(Third Eucharistic Prayer, Roman Rite)

By this same Holy Spirit, we are divinized, transformed, "mercified" (if I may coin a word), to be living Eucharist, members of the Body of Christ. By this transformation we radiate His mercy.

This transformation is a gradual process as we are nourished by the Body and Blood of the Lord and "become what we eat"! (St. Augustine, and a good biochemical principle). This transformation takes time and repeated reception of Holy Eucharist, and repeated and extended times of "radiation therapy" and gazing upon Him. Gradually, we begin to radiate the mercy of the Father as Jesus did, and live the Eucharist.

We are challenged and called to be **living Eucharist**, so that all who see our light (Mt 5:14-17) may give glory to God; that seeing the radiance of God's mercy in us, all may be confronted by the sign of contradiction to our age and see the answer to our crisis in the Church and world.

Lord, fill me with Your mercy, irradiate me with Your mercy, transform me by Your mercy, that I may radiate Your mercy to the world as living Eucharist!

　　　　　　　　　　　　　　　　　　Father George

The following titles, also written by Fr. Kosicki and published by Faith Publishing Company, may be ordered from The Riehle Foundation.

ICONS OF MERCY
Meditations for the ordained and those in religious life. 170 pgs. $6.00

WHAT'S IT ALL ABOUT?
Meditations on the meaning of life.
64 pgs. $3.00

SPIRITUAL WARFARE
The existence of Satan and his influence on our age. 156 pgs. $5.00

The Riehle Foundation is a non-profit, tax-exempt publisher and distributor of Catholic books and materials, and also distributes books for Faith Publishing Company. Donations for books, though not required, are appreciated. Suggested values are indicated above. Write to:

THE RIEHLE FOUNDATION
P.O. BOX 7
MILFORD, OHIO 45150

Faith Publishing Company

Faith Publishing Company has been organized as a service for the publishing and distribution of materials that reflect Christian values, and in particular the teachings of the Catholic Church.

It is dedicated to publication of only those materials that reflect such values.

Faith Publishing Company also publishes books for The Riehle Foundation. The Foundation is a non-profit, tax-exempt producer and distributor of Catholic books and materials world-wide, and also supplies hospital and prison ministries, churches and mission organizations.

For more information on the publications of Faith Publishing Company, contact:

Faith Publishing Company

P.O. BOX 237
MILFORD, OHIO 45150